John Orrell Lever

Austria

Her Position and Prospects

John Orrell Lever

Austria
Her Position and Prospects

ISBN/EAN: 9783743329409

Manufactured in Europe, USA, Canada, Australia, Japa

Cover: Foto ©ninafisch / pixelio.de

Manufactured and distributed by brebook publishing software
(www.brebook.com)

John Orrell Lever

Austria

AUSTRIA;

HER POSITION

AND

PROSPECTS.

BY JOHN ORRELL LEVER, M.P.

Price 2s. 6d.

FOURTH THOUSAND.

LONDON:

EDWARD STANFORD, 6, CHARING CROSS.

1861.

CONTENTS.

"In short, the empire may be said to have as yet wanted almost
" entirely the stimulus to industry arising from communication by
" water, from a universally established steam-communication, and, above
" all, from a liberal commercial legislation."—*Encyclopædia Britannica*,
Eighth Edition, 1854.

"The low rank held by Austria among commercial nations, whether
" as a producer or as a consumer, has long struck every one acquainted
" with the resources of the empire ;   and the more the subject is
" examined, the greater becomes the surprise at the slight benefit which
" has been derived from their natural advantages, by a population num-
" bering above 38,000,000 of souls, placed in a country bordering on one
" side some of the most active and industrious States of Germany, and
" traversed by one of the largest and most easily navigable streams of
" Europe, which seemed especially calculated to secure to Austrian
" enterprise the advantages of the lucrative markets of the Levant."—
Fenn's Compendium of the English and Foreign Funds.

CHAPTER I.

The subject to which I now desire to direct public
attention, possesses more than ordinary importance.
It has reference to the capabilities of a great and
powerful empire, and one that has not hitherto
received the attention it deserves. In considering
this question in all its bearings, the reader will be
constrained to admit, that it is not a little remarkable
that the importance of the Austrian dominions, as an
active and increasing market for manufactured goods,
should have been completely overlooked. She is now
a producer to a large extent, and can provide us with
raw material in great abundance. Yet our usually
keen and far-seeing merchants and manufacturers,
who hunt up buyers in every part of the world, seem
to have been totally blind to the capabilities of this
near neighbour, and to the advantages to be derived
from the extensive use of the productions and commodities which she possesses in such quantities.
These turned to proper account would give employ-

ment, and thereby the means of obtaining cheap food, to our industrial population. The wealth lying undeveloped in the widely extending plains of Austria may be converted into blessings, not only for England, but for other European countries. And the increased intercommunication and intercourse, to which the efforts necessary for this development would give rise, must constitute the best guarantees for the preservation of tranquillity, and the progress of civilization.

The gold fields of California, Australasia, and British Columbia, have attracted thousands of enterprising spirits from all quarters of the globe, and have necessarily led to an extension of commerce beyond our most glowing anticipations. Yet whilst every effort is made to utilize those mines of wealth in distant regions, we should not neglect the gold fields nearer home, which only require the application of well directed enterprise and industry, in order to yield a rich return.

Being thoroughly impressed with the importance which a right understanding of the great commercial capabilities of Austria, the neighbour and ancient ally of this country, must prove to the British public, I am induced to lay before them the results of my inquiries, during recent visits of some duration to different parts of that empire. I am strongly convinced that if even a slight idea of the wide field for enterprise that lies open to them, is once entertained by our commercial classes, the opportunity will be no longer neglected.

The development of the immense resources of Austria is a vital question. It is one that largely affects the interests of more than sixty millions of people, and its prompt solution is, in my judgment, of great moment not only directly to Austria and Great Britain, but indirectly to the whole of Europe.

Moreover in the present crisis in European affairs, aggravated by the unfortunate turn that events have taken in the United States of America, it is highly essential that just and definite information, respecting the character and position of the Austrian empire, should be placed before the British people. Questions have arisen, which an accurate knowledge of the past history of this empire, will alone enable us to understand. The information once obtained and digested, whilst it serves as a key both to the past and to the present, will also throw light upon the future. It will, in fact, afford the only satisfactory answer to the oft-repeated inquiry, as to the part that Austria will henceforth be called upon to play, in the great European confederacy.

Recent events which have had the effect of directing public attention to Austria, have revealed the misconception that prevails, even in educated circles in this country, respecting her character, position and policy. Little is really known of the nature of her political and social institutions, of the extent of her resources, of the amount of her natural productions, of the condition of her manufactures, or of her influence for good or for evil, in the councils of the world. In plain terms, the general public of Great Britain, are not in possession of correct information upon these matters. The consequence is, that the acts of Austria have been distorted, her policy has been misrepresented, and her importance under-rated.

Nor will this unsatisfactory state of affairs excite surprise in the mind of the candid reader, if he reflects for a moment on the sources to which prevailing notions respecting Austria, her government, her people, her institutions, and her capabilities, may be traced. Those who are interested in producing unfavourable impressions, have been permitted to deal with her history exactly as they pleased. Political exiles, and foreign assailants have, by continual clamour, completely drowned the voice of truth. Englishmen have contented themselves with garbled statements, which have necessarily produced an abundant crop of the most erroneous views and conclusions. Hence they have regarded the Austrian Empire in that light only, which served the purposes of these interested guides. They have, and perhaps when everything is taken into consideration, it must be admitted not unnaturally, permitted themselves to fall into errors almost childish in their character, respecting this most powerful state, from whose independent friendship and honourable alliance, our statesmen, our manufacturers, our commercial and our labouring classes might, each in their particular sphere, derive incalculable advantages.

One specious method used to allure the British people from the real points at issue in the controversy, has been by raising an absurd cry respecting the nationalities. The word is seldom employed without being accompanied by a censure upon the course pursued by Austria. Yet what does this clamour respecting the nationalities actually mean? It becomes when fairly examined, more an European than an Austrian question. If we reflect upon, and trace the progress of any one of the great powers, we shall find the principle of the nationalities sacrified at almost every stage in its history. Each member of the European confederacy has been formed by the gradual subjugation of different races to one strong and central authority; and thus have mighty empires been moulded from the fragmentary materials of numerous lesser states. To this rule there are no exceptions. Every European power, at this moment in existence, has been formed by a fusion of what are termed the nationalities. (*a.*)

Austria has acquired her extensive possessions by

(*a*) 1 am pleased, whilst this pamphlet is passing through the press, to avail myself of the opportunity of quoting the following arguments, in suport of this view, from an article in the "Times" of Friday, May 3rd, 1861. The writer says: "The great difficulty lies in the singular "composition of Austria. True, other States have also been formed "by a fusion of nationalities. It is the universal process in such matters, "and none but those who have studied the subject can have any conception "of the extent to which provincial aggregation has been carried in the "manufacture of great Monarchies. Not only are France and England, for "instance, made up of such pieces, but each piece itself was first made up of "twenty smaller pieces. There is hardly an English county which does not "represent communities once independent of each other. By the successive "consolidation and amalgamation of these ingredients mighty States were "created; and why, therefore, should not the unity of Austria be estab- "lished in a similar manner?"

the same absorbing process adopted by other empires. Although she has been most severely and unceasingly condemned, she has but followed the general practice. It may indeed be true that some of her subjects do not understand the language in which the affairs of the empire are administered ; yet many of the subjects of France, of Russia, and even of Great Britain itself, to say nothing of those of the minor principalities and powers, are in the same condition. Although this fusion may have reached a more advanced stage in other countries than in Austria, it is daily going forward, and supplies the impartial mind with a complete vindication of the course pursued by her, and the best refutation of the shallow theories which prejudiced writers have so widely circulated.

The demand for the revival of the nationalities, and the consequent separation of the various empires of Europe into their component parts, is the watchword of revolution. It strikes at the liberties of every people, and at the foundations of every state. Let this subversive principle be inexorably carried out, and the world must at once retrograde ten centuries. Europe would consist of weak and wrangling states, instead of well-organized empires. Every landmark would be removed, the definition of boundaries would become impossible, and fierce contests would rage upon innumerable frontiers.

What is this outcry then, but an attempt to destroy at one blow the progress in civilization achieved since the overthrow of the old Roman dominion? When that disruption occurred, tribes wandered from place to place, the strong seeking to enrich themselves at the expense of the weak. At that gloomy period in the annals of the world, the nationalities flourished in full vigour. Their revival would be the signal for the dismemberment of Europe. There would be a separation of the present elements without the most remote prospect of a reconstruction. The modern system which has worked so well in preserving the balance of power, and in securing the happiness of millions, would be at once destroyed ; and a revolutionary spirit could not fail to obtain the ascendant.

I am induced to allude to this question of the nationalities, because it illustrates in a forcible manner the unsound, and the unjust line of argument, so generally pursued in treating of Austria. Her policy in this matter has been denounced as though it were something of her own invention, whereas it is identical with that which all other European powers have adopted, and are at this moment following out, in dealing with the varied elements of which their respective empires are composed.

When we consider the ignorance that prevails amongst nations respecting the character, policy, and condition of their immediate neighbours, we cannot feel surprise at the absence of any well-directed efforts on the part of the British public to obtain authentic information with regard to Austria. The case is by no means an exceptional one. France itself, whose northern shores are within sight of our own, is to this hour a land of mystery and of fable, to a large portion of the community. During the present year, a French writer who visited England, as he states, to obtain information for the instruction of his countrymen, has published a book which is inaccurate in almost every particular relating to Her Majesty's subjects, their customs and institutions. The French people, (I allude of course to the mass of the population,) know little more of us, than they do of the inhabitants of some island in the great southern ocean. Why therefore should the want of information respecting Austria, that prevails amongst the public of Great Britain, create astonishment?

Railroads, steamships, and electric telegraphs are doubtless producing, and must continue to produce, great changes in this state of things. Happily, even so far as Austria is concerned, a commencement has been made ; intercourse is increasing, and trade is springing up. Commerce, after all the great civilizer, is more generally appreciated and we may reasonably hope that by its agency not only the French and English people will become better acquainted, but what is no less important, that Austria will also be brought into closer connection with us.

CHAPTER II.

A statesman called upon to name the richest possessions of a country, would unhesitatingly refer to its natural and mineral productions, and the energies of its people by which these productions are rendered available for the every day requirements of life, and are thereby converted into sources of national prosperity and independence. The former constitute the capital of the state; the latter the healthy activity which converts that capital into wealth.

On these points I therefore believe it to be of importance that I should give my readers some information. It is but reasonable that before I attempt to shew what Austria can do, I should explain what she really is at this moment. It is not sufficient to say that she is powerful; it is necessary that I should point out in what that power consists. The task will not I think prove so difficult as may at first be supposed.

If we glance at the map of Europe we shall find that the place occupied by the Austrian dominions is in every respect highly favourable. Her territories central and well situated, stretch away to the South, finding an outlet in the Adriatic Sea, the principal arm of the Mediterranean. Her coast line, several hundred miles in extent, contains numerous harbours and havens easy of access, suitable for the equipment and maintenance of fleets both for commercial and defensive purposes.

Her climate is naturally, from her wide extent of territory, varied, but on the whole genial, and in every respect favourable to the operations of agriculture. The soil is remarkable for its fertility; and the facility with which large crops are produced will surprise those, who know with what exertion and toil, such results are obtained by ourselves.

A brief recapitulation of the articles grown in abundance in the Austrian empire will afford some idea of her capabilities. As a grain producing country she occupies a high rank. All kinds of corn are cultivated in large quantities. Of wheat, the staple of human life, she not only grows sufficient for her own population, but also to supply largely by export the demands of other markets ; and this is accomplished almost without effort, that is to say, without an attempt to develope the resources of her fertile plains to anything approaching their full power. The immense crops produced throughout Hungary and Galicia have justly caused those provinces to be called the granaries of Europe. Nor are the supplies obtained from Bohemia, Silesia,

Moravia, and the plains of the lower Danube less important. Potatoes, ordinary vegetables, and fruit of every kind abound in all parts of the empire. The vine flourishes luxuriantly in Hungary, whilst in the southern provinces bordering on the Mediteranean, the olive, the orange, and many tropical plants are cultivated with success. Rice is also grown, and the quantity planted is rapidly increasing.

Plants, constituting the raw material for manufacturing purposes, are also included amongst the staple productions of the Austrian empire. Flax is grown in every province. Hungary, Moravia, Galicia, and the Southern portions of the country furnish supplies of white hemp. The hop is found in abundance in Bohemia; the indigo plant has been recently introduced under very favourable circumstances in Dalmatia; and immense quantities of tobacco are produced in Hungary, and in other provinces. Maize, beet-root, and rape-seed may be added to the varied list.

Persons interested in ship building, or in any occupation in which well seasoned timber is required, will readily admit its value. With this material Austria is largely supplied. Her forests, which cover a space of nearly one hundred thousand square miles, appear almost inexhaustible. From them supplies of the finest quality are obtained; not to speak of turpentine, tar, charcoal, and potash, all of which are to be had in abundance. As a wine producing country, Austria is not behind any in Europe. Four-fifths of the wine manufactured in the Austrian empire come from Hùngary; and the produce, both as regards character and quality, will not suffer from comparison even with the wines of France. Some of the superior growths only require to be known, to rise in public estimation, and consequently in price; while the ordinary wines are calculated to enter largely into our future consumption. From want of proper facilities of transport, much of the wine produced does not even command a price equal in amount to the value of the cask in which it is contained.

Over territories so extensive, numerous herds of cattle and flocks of sheep are necessarily scattered. Though sufficient attention has not been paid to the breeding of domestic animals, yet they are found in great numbers. Special care is devoted to the breeding of horses. Goats and swine abound in all parts of the empire. Considerable quantities of both the finer and the coarser kinds of wool, are obtained from the numerous flocks reared in nearly every province. The skins of wild animals also form an element in the resources of this country; whilst her fisheries afford occupation, as well as food, to the inhabitants of several districts.

For mineral wealth, Austria may be said to stand almost alone amongst the nations of the eastern hemisphere. Every mineral except platinum, is to be obtained in one or other of her provinces. Iron abounds in every part of the country. In addition to the precious metals silver and gold, quicksilver, lead, copper, zinc, and tin, are to be found. The useful earths may also be noticed. Stone for architectural purposes, clay for porcelain, marble, gypsum, and chalk are abundant. Nor must we forget precious stones, in a country whence the Hungarian opal, and the Bohemian garnet are obtained.

Her salt mines are perhaps the most extensive in Europe, and coal exists in large quantities. To the latter little attention has as yet been directed, in consequence of the abundance of wood, and the want of facilities of transport. It is, however, evident from certain indications, that Austria possesses coal beds of a superior quality, and to a much greater extent, than even persons well qualified to give an opinion have any idea.

I have thus alluded to the productions of Austria, because I deem it most advisable to define her real capabilities, before I attempt to show in what manner they have been employed. These constitute her stock in trade; they are the weapons placed in the hands of her people to enable them to make their way in the world. Some countries but little favoured in this respect have achieved renown. The energy of their inhabitants has compensated for a sterile soil, and an ungenial climate. Such advantages therefore, as those which I have thus briefly referred to, are mighty agents; and when used with diligence and properly directed, must become real elements of power. They tend to make people happy, and nations great; and have been bestowed by an all-wise providence for a beneficent purpose.

Having thus stated the principal resources of this great empire, I pass to another question; namely, how Austria has employed these important instruments of advancement and prosperity.

CHAPTER III.

DEVELOPMENT ; OR THE USE MADE BY AUSTRIA OF HER RESOURCES.

How have the inhabitants of the provinces of which the Austrian empire is composed, employed these mighty agents,—these varied elements of wealth, civilization, and power? What have these thirty-nine millions of people done to prove their proper appreciation of these advantages ? I have pointed out the capital which they possess, let us now see the results produced. From the foregoing statements some idea may be formed of what might have been effected. It is not, therefore, unreasonable to ask, " What has in reality been done? "

This great empire, composed of different provinces, occupies an area of about two hundred and fifty thousand square miles. It is inhabited, but not too thickly, by different races, some peaceably inclined and others warlike, yet all attached to their homes. From a carefully prepared estimate, it appears that there are in England 240 inhabitants to every square mile ; in France 175 ; while in Austria the number does not exceed 153. This calculation shows, that although the Austrian territory is not overcrowded, it contains a population sufficiently numerous to give full development to its capabilities, and to its resources.

The position of an empire of such an extent and the general character of its surface, are important considerations in an inquiry of this nature.

Austria unfortunately ranks below other nations, so far as her means of intercommunication amongst her own people, and her facilities for intercourse with the inhabitants of other countries are concerned. Her territories, generally of a hilly character, are traversed by three mountain chains, the Alps, the Carpathians, and the Swedetes, besides several lesser ranges. Swamps and morasses present formidable obstacles to traffic in many provinces ; whilst dense forests form impenetrable barriers in other directions. Before agriculture could make any advance, before manu- factures could flourish, or, in fact, anything like extensive trade spring into existence, means of inter- communication were required. It must not, however, be supposed that the rulers of Austria have been insensible to this necessity. Some 20,000 miles of highway have been constructed, and above 100 moun- tain passes have been rendered available for traffic—I might, perhaps, add, within the present century. The Alpine roads over the Stelvio pass, the Splugen, and the Semering, may be classed amongst the most important public works of modern times ; and although these highways have not, from the costly nature of the transport, been much used for heavy goods, yet they afford very great facilities for intercourse between different provinces, providing in addition, routes for the transmission of mails, and the conveyance of light and valuable goods.

For the transport of agricultural and other produce, manufactured and heavy articles, canals have been constructed, and rivers rendered available. Yet in a mountainous country like Austria, it would be impossible to introduce a regular net-work of canals. The great advance therefore has been in the formation of railways, and the employment of steam power for inland navigation, where the rivers or canals permitted its application.

In 1841, the Austrian Government commenced the construction of railways, for the purpose of connecting the various parts of the empire. Above 3000 miles of line have since been opened, and other important links in the system, are now being rapidly completed.

Thus slowly, but steadily, have numerous obstacles to general intercourse been removed. Mountains have been rendered passable, streams have been bridged, swamps and morasses drained, good roads have been constructed, and water carriage encouraged and promoted. Several impediments to free circulation within the limits of the empire, have in consequence disappeared, and although much still remains to be done, many great works have been constructed, the complete success of which, cannot fail to serve as a guide, as well as an incentive, to future exertion.

The progress of Austrian agriculture has not been by any means so marked, as might have been anticipated. It is not however in the backward state which some writers represent. Favoured alike in soil and in climate, the Austrian agriculturist has not felt the urgent necessity of seeking the aid of modern invention, or of taking advantage of modern machinery. The productive powers of the land, are not tested to the utmost. Yet the agriculturist is beginning to appreciate the advantages of a large export trade. The opening of railways, producing cheaper rates of carriage, serves as a further inducement to exertion. And in some parts of the empire, a very striking improvement may be observed. The land, for instance, from the frontiers of Saxony to Vienna, affords a specimen of high cultivation, that will bear comparison with the best districts in other European countries. From a recent calculation, it would appear that the approximate value of agricultural produce in England, in France, and in Austria, is £276,000,000, £160,000,000, and £120,000,000.

The manufactured productions of Austria are principally linen, woollen, and cotton fabrics, hardware, silk, glass, paper, leather, and sugar. In many articles, more especially of luxury, the skill displayed and the results produced are remarkable. Yet her manufactures, like her agriculture, admit of considerable extension and development ; and in both, the introduction of modern machinery would lead to important changes. At present many manufactured articles are produced piecemeal, and frequently by hand. The consequence is, that they are sometimes much dearer than at Paris or in London.

The various provinces of which the Austrian empire is composed, have not contributed their quota to the extraordinary supplies of corn, that have been required for consumption in European countries, during the last few years. Her exports of grain are not by any means equivalent to her power of production. She possesses over and above the means of providing for her own population, an undeveloped power of contributing, to an immense extent, to the various markets of Europe, and of thus taking her place as one of the largest producers of the great staple of human life. Hitherto, the owners and the tillers of the soil in Austria, have not derived that return, either for capital or labour, which must follow the adoption of the improved methods of agriculture to which I have already referred, and the creation of those additional facilities of transport so much needed.

The capabilities of the soil are not in fact fully developed. Nor have the people availed themselves of the advantages they possess as the producers of raw material for various manufactures. For purposes of food, or of clothing, corn, maize, hops, hemp and flax might be exported by the inhabitants of Austria to a much greater extent than at present.

Her vast forests, affording abundance of excellent timber, are comparatively speaking neglected ; whilst no efforts, worthy of the name, have been made to adapt the Hungarian wines to the English taste, or to bring them into the English markets. Wine of excellent quality is literally wasted from the want of a little management. The people of Austria might, in this matter, learn a lesson from the wine growers at the Cape of Good Hope. In spite of the numerous obstacles with which they have had to contend, they have furnished supplies of sound wine, at a cheap rate, for our home consumption, and this has been accomplished in a colony, which is separated from the mother country by a long sea passage.

It will be unnecessary for me to go through every item in the list, or I might refer to similar neglect of many other natural riches of this empire, as well as of her minerals and useful earths. I believe that I have said enough to shew that the Austrian people have not turned their immense resources to the best account. I cannot however refrain from referring to two important minerals, which she possesses in abundance, and which have been strangely neglected. I allude to coal and iron. These it is unnecessary to say have been chiefly instrumental in raising England to her present high position amongst the nations of the world; these, by the industry of the English people, have been converted into sources of wealth and of influence. Yet disregarding this example, the coal and iron of Austria have only been employed to a very limited extent. And as they are the essentials of manufacturing success, I need scarcely add that in Austria manufactures are not very numerous.

Hitherto Austria has not made the best use of her opportunities for advancement and prosperity. Her people have not derived from the various elements of wealth, civilization and power, with which the empire abounds, the results they are capable of producing. They have buried their treasure instead of using it, and to this many of the inconveniences from which they have long suffered, must be attributed.

CHAPTER IV.

FACTS AND FIGURES.

The following extracts from the returns of British Exports will give an idea of the position occupied by Austria as a trader in our markets. I have selected the years 1857 and 1858, because they were years of peace between the Crimean struggle, and the war in the plains of Lombardy. The returns are of the declared real value of the exports of the produce of the United Kingdom sent in each year to the countries mentioned in the List.

	1857. £	1858. £	Total for 1857 & 58 £
U. States	18,985,939	14,491,448	33,477,387
E. Indies	13,079,653	18,283,852	31,363,505
Australia	11,632,524	10,463,032	22,095,556
Hanse Towns	9,595,962	9,031,877	18,627,839
Holland	6,384,394	5,473,312	11,857,706
France & Algeria	6,232,764	4,884,164	11,116,928
Brazil	5,541,710	3,984,817	9,526,527
Turkey	3,107,401	4,255,612	7,363,013
Russia	3,098,819	3,092,499	6,191,318
Canada	2,467,810	1,737,751	4,205,561
Spain	2,012,528	2,071,219	4,083,747
Egypt	1,899,289	1,985,829	3,885,118
Spanish W. Indies	1,865,667	1,877,072	3,742,739

	1857. £	1858. £	Total for 1857 & 58. £
Prussia	1,741,044	1,956,199	3,697,243
British W. India Islands	1,830.413	1,792,323	3,622,736
Cape of Good Hope and Natal	1,860,638	1,703,397	3,564,035
Belgium	1,727,204	1,815,257	3,542,461
China	1,728,885	1,730,778	3,459,663
Hanover	1,637,741	1,640,189	3,277,930
Portugal	1,458,321	1,432,238	2,890,559
Two Sicilies	1,088,982	1,569,166	2,658,148
Chili	1,520,678	1,117,580	2,638,258
Sardinia	1,350,210	1,174,580	2,524,790
Austria (a)	1,112,559	1,298,199	2,410,758

Notwithstanding her proximity to England, (now within forty-eight hours by sea and railway, and instantaneous telegraphic communication), and the extent of her territories, during the years 1857 and 1858, twenty-three states, and many of them of small dimensions, took a larger quantity of British exports than Austria.

If we examine other statistics, we shall find that no modern state has advanced so slowly as Austria. She has permitted other members of the European family to leave her far behind in a struggle for supremacy, in which many advantages were in her favour. It will be sufficient, in order to elucidate my state-

(a) The Exports that pass through the Hanseatic and other ports, and thus find their way into Austria, are of course not included in these figures. This is an uncertain element in exports that it is impossible to ascertain with any degree of accuracy.

ment, to institute a comparison in certain particulars between Austria, France, and England, three of the five leading powers of Europe.

The extent of the three empires may be thus summarily stated—Austria occupies an area of about 254,000 square miles, with a population of about 39,000,000 (*a*) ; France occupies an area of about 205,000 square miles, with a population of about 36,000,000 ; and Great Britain and Ireland comprise an area of about 125,000 square miles (*b*), with a population of about 30,000,000 souls.

Let us now endeavour to ascertain how the inhabitants of these different states have turned the various advantages which they possess to account.

As the first item bearing upon the question I will take the amount of revenue raised by each of these states. In order to make the comparison as fair as possible let us select two years, 1852 and 1858, the former a year previous to the war in the Crimea, and the latter the year before the Italian struggle. By consulting the best authorities we find that the

(*a*) Previous to this cession of Lombardy to Sardinia, the Austrian Empire comprised an area of 254,548 square miles, with a population of 39,411,309. I have adhered to that calculation, as the dismemberment had not taken place at the period to which these estimates refer. Lombardy comprises 8,235 square miles, with a population of 3,009,505.

(*b*) The actual numbers are :—

						Area.	Population.
England and Wales	..	..	..	..		58,320	17,927,609
Ireland	..	..	..	..	...	35,511	8,175,124
Scotland	..	..	..	..	..	31,324	2,888,742
Total	..	..	..	..	..	125,155	28,991,475

revenue for the year 1852, in the three states, stood as follows:—

	Area in sq. mls.	Population.	Revenue.
Austria	254,000	39,000,000	£26,636,511
France	205,000	36,000,000	59,493,799
Gt. Britain	125,000	30,000,000	53,210,071

Thus France, with a territory smaller in area by one-fifth, raised, in 1852, a revenue exceeding that of Austria by £32,857,288.

During the same year the revenue of Great Britain, of which the area is not quite one half the extent of that of Austria, and with 9,000,000 less inhabitants was £26,573,560 in excess of the revenue contributed by the inhabitants of the Austrian empire.

In other words, the revenue of France more than doubled, and the revenue of Great Britain almost exactly doubled, in the year 1852, that of Austria, which both in extent of territory and in amount of population, surpassed both kingdoms.

Each inhabitant in England, contributed on the average £1 15s. 5½d.; each inhabitant in France contributed £1 13s. 0½d.; and each inhabitant in Austria contributed only 13s. 7¾d. to the revenue of the respective empires in 1852.

The lapse of six years brings us to 1858, when the revenue in the three states was as follows:—

	Area in sq. mls.	Population.	Revenue.
Austria	254,000	39,000,000	£28,254,072
France	205,000	36,000,000	74,680,000
Gt. Britain	125,000	30,000,000	61,812,555

Thus the increase in the revenues of the three states, in the year 1858, as compared with the sums raised for this purpose in 1852, amounted in France to £15,186,201; in Great Britain to £8,602,484; and in Austria to only £1,617,561.

Let us mark the change which followed this interval of six years; the revenue of France became nearly three times that of Austria, and the revenue of Great Britain more than double.

The contribution of taxes for each subject in France was, on the average in 1852, £1 13s. $0\frac{1}{2}$d., which became £2 1s. $5\frac{3}{4}$d. in 1858, while in England the average increased from £1 15s. $5\frac{1}{2}$d. to £2 1s. $2\frac{1}{2}$d. But in Austria the increase was so trifling, notwithstanding the expenditure incurred during the Russian campaign, as to be scarcely worthy of remark. The average in 1852, was 13s. $7\frac{3}{4}$d. per head, and in 1858 it was 14s. $5\frac{3}{4}$d.

As far, therefore, as revenue is concerned, it is evident that, taking extent, number of population, and resources into consideration, double the amount at present collected in the Austrian dominions might be easily obtained, were her capabilities fairly developed. And this might be accomplished without prejudice to any interest, and without placing burdens on the people, which they are unable to bear.

It is also worthy of notice that, although the amount of revenue raised by Austria is, when compared with the efforts made by Great Britain or

France, so small, the debt of the Austrian empire is by no means excessive. In the year 1856, the funded and unfunded debt of Great Britain, amounted to £803,913,694. The public funded debt of France amounted in the same year to £302,321,632; whilst the debt of the Austrian empire did not exceed £241,700,000.

It may be urged that for many years there has been a balance on the wrong side, between the receipts and expenditure of Austria. The fact, however, only affords a more striking proof of the necessity that exists for that active cultivation of the resources of the empire, which would place her commercially and financially in a position to which she is entitled, and re-establish her credit on the various Exchanges of Europe.

I have already shown to what an extent Austria was a purchaser in the markets of Great Britain in the years 1857 and 1858. It may be desirable to carry the investigation a little further, in order to obtain some idea of the amount of her own exports and imports, and the relation they bear to the exports and imports of Great Britain, and of France.

For this purpose let us take the year 1857, of which the returns give the following results :—

	IMPORTS.	£
Austria	... ...	26,806,252
France	... ...	107,560,060
Great Britain	...	187,844,441

D

EXPORTS.

		£
Austria ...	...	28,745,845
France ...	...	104,572,000
Great Britain	...	146,174,300

While the balance of trade in favour of Austria amounted in 1857 to £1,939,593, the gross amount of her exports and imports, was only one-fourth of the gross amount of the exports and imports of France, and only one-sixth of the gross amount of the exports and imports of Great Britain.

CHAPTER V.

A moment's reflection will convince the reader that a clear knowledge of the position of Austria, especially at this moment, is a matter of great importance to this country. It is a question that deeply concerns the interests of all classes. We have more to gain from the possession of sound and correct information, and more to lose from remaining uninformed, than may at first strike even candid, and unprejudiced minds.

Austria during the last two years has undergone a great change. One of her fairest provinces has been wrested from her, and important reforms in her system of government have been inaugurated. In defiance of many assertions to the contrary put forward by her opponents, she has really entered upon the path of constitutional government, and she has done so, with extraordinary success. The Reichsrath, or great Council of the Empire, was re-established by patent, dated March 5th, 1860. The condition of the empire, the necessity for judicious changes, and the form those changes were to

D 2

assume, became the questions for its deliberations. The Emperor in this crisis, surrounded by the wisest counsellors, endeavoured to ascertain the course, which it was his duty to pursue, and his acts although bold have been temperate. The diploma of the 20th of October, followed as the natural result of the investigation and deliberations of the Reichsrath. Taxation, the making of laws, and all questions of imperial policy are placed under the control of the imperial legislature, whilst to the provincial diets, the regulation of subjects that relate exclusively to the provinces are entrusted. Thus constitutional government, on a broad and liberal basis is established. This is not a mere juggling with freedom, the shadow without the substance, or a solemn mockery, but a real reform; and the manner in which it has been received by the people of Austria, proves that its advantages are clearly appreciated. Keeping in view the imperative necessity of preserving the unity of the empire, the government have laboured zealously at the good work of restoration. They have not suffered themselves to be deluded by senseless cries for changes that lead to revolution, but have endeavoured to obtain practical results from a thoroughly sound and practical reform.

Many persons whose opinions are entitled to respect, are in the habit of condemning the Emperor of Austria, and of regarding him as a bigot or a tyrant. I certainly do not pretend to say that he has always acted wisely, or that he has been free from error. Like other rulers he has committed mistakes. I venture, however, to assert, and I feel confident that no person possessing accurate information on the subject, will attempt to contradict me, that neither amongst rulers nor subjects, can there be found in Europe, at this moment, a man more earnest in his efforts to do justice. This has been, and is the great object of his life.

The connection between the ruler and the people in Austria is peculiar, and bears a strong resemblance to the relations that have existed between the British nation and their Sovereign, since our most gracious Queen ascended the throne. The Emperor of Austria is regarded as the father of his people. By a thousand pleasing traits is this sympathy, this intimate relationship displayed; and it is extended towards every member of the royal family. It would be impossible for me to convey to my readers, even a feeble impression of the grief excited amongst the people of Vienna, and the neighbourhood, by the indisposition of the Empress. They lamented the cause, which rendered her short absence from home, necessary, as sincerely as if it had affected some loved inmate of their own homes.

The members of the royal family of Austria are moreover, the most earnest advocates of advancement and salutary changes. They have laboured in various departments of the state, to remedy abuses, and to discover the means by which the stability of the empire may be secured.

In their recent attempts at reform, the Emperor and his family have been aided by zealous and enlightened ministers. Foremost amongst them is Count Rechberg, a liberal and practical statesman. And what is of deeper interest to this country, he is a great admirer of our institutions, and a warm supporter of an alliance with England.

M. De Schmerling, one of his colleagues, is a man possessing much experience and extraordinary resolution. Devoted to the cause of liberty, he is ever prompt to oppose any movement calculated in the slightest degree to disturb that equilibrium, the preservation of which is so essential for the safety of the state. The finance minister, M. Von Plener, deservedly enjoys a high reputation and is believed to possess not only the necessary ability, but the independence and the boldness required to shake off olden trammels. His natural inclination will induce him to adopt the more modern system, by which alone the resources of Austria can be fully developed, and the elasticity of her finances restored.

I must also mention Baron Vay, to whom the administration of the affairs of Hungary is entrusted. This upright statesman deservedly enjoys the confidence of the inhabitants of that important portion of the country.

I might easily extend the list, but I think I have

stated enough to shew that the government of Austria is at present in safe hands. The Emperor, his counsellors and ministers have undertaken a difficult task, and what they have already achieved, may be accepted as an earnest of even greater exertions for the future. Austria, therefore, is no longer what she was. She has made some rapid strides in the right direction. This has been accomplished, it is true, without noisy parade or boisterous self-adulation. There have been no senseless appeals to Europe, or to the civilized world. She has set her house in order, in sober quietness, and perfectly satisfied with the result, she leaves the good work to speak for itself. This it must be admitted is the best sign of success. More than once, even of late years, constitutions framed amid a wild outburst of feverish excitement, have suddenly fallen to pieces, overwhelming their architects and supporters in one common destruction.

Let the enemies of Austria say what they please, from one extremity of the empire to the other, a strong determination to retrieve the errors of the past prevails. No state in which the sovereign and the government display such spirit, such determination and such faith in their own powers and in their own institutions, has cause for apprehension. They have boldly undertaken a great work, they intend to accomplish it, and under these circumstances, failure becomes impossible.

CHAPTER VI.

THE GREAT DESIDERATUM.

About one hundred and sixty years ago, a man of stalwart form and somewhat noble aspect, might have been seen, sometimes watching and sometimes taking part in the operations of ship-building, carried on in Deptford dock-yard. From the numerous attendants that followed his steps, and the ceremony with which he was everywhere received, it must have been apparent, even to casual observers, that he was no ordinary personage. Had any curious spectator made more particular inquiries, he would doubtless have been told, that the mysterious being in whose movements he took such an interest, was Peter the Great, Czar of Muscovy. His informant would probably have added that he was learning the art of ship-building. This, however, would have given but a feeble idea of his real mission; he was in fact founding an empire.

At the time of Peter's visit to England, the whole maritime trade of Russia was carried on at Archangel, a port which, as Macaulay (a) observes, "had

(a) In the fifth volume of the History of England, recently published, an account is given of this port, and of the rise of the Russian Navy.

been created, and was supported by adventurers from our island." No sooner did this sagacious monarch find the reins of government in his hands, than he perceived that Russia could not become influential as a leading European state, unless she possessed a navy. Had he been easily daunted, his limited sea-board, and the disposition of his countrymen, would have been sufficient to deter him from making an effort to create one. Russia was then without sea-coast or harbours, and the people hated the very name of the sea. But Peter, like all men who have a mission to fulfil, was not to be thus easily daunted. By working in the dock-yards, and acting the sailor wherever he went, he triumphed over the prejudices of his subjects. He felt satisfied that if a navy was once established, additional harbours and sea-ports must rapidly follow.

To this determination on the part of her greatest sovereign, Russia owes her power. Had it not been for his forethought and perseverance, she might have remained a weak member of the family of European nations; shut up, and little known in all but impenetrable regions of frost and snow. But his ardent spirit burst through the icy barrier, and the Russia of modern times, stretches far away into southern latitudes, and boasts of shores washed by different seas. At the port of Archangel, to which I have referred, inaccessible on account of the ice during eight months of the year, a navy was formed, and a maritime trade established. To that solitary port in the far north, others, in more congenial latitudes have since been added, and Russia now ranks third amongst the great naval powers of Europe.

The opportunity which Russia improved has been up to the present time neglected by Austria. She has witnessed the repeated exertions of her powerful neighbour, without having been induced to follow the example, virtually retiring from a struggle, in which everything was in her favour.

From the foregoing remarks, it will not be difficult to understand, the principal requirements of Austria;—the reasons why her strength is not put forth, why her influence is in a certain sense circumscribed. The want of a fleet paralyses her trade and places her at a disadvantage with other nations of Europe. Take the examples of Carthage, of the Grecian States, and of Rome, in the ancient world; what would they have been without their fleets? To what did Venice, did Genoa, did Portugal, Spain, or Holland owe their commercial position? If this was the case in past times when navigation was difficult, and its principles were imperfectly understood, how much greater must be the value of a navy, now that the sea has become the highway of nations, and ships are propelled by steam?

In this respect the rulers and the people of Austria have been blind to their own interests. They ought to have omitted no opportunity of creating a navy, both for commercial, and defensive purposes. The work, which Russia has so well accomplished, commencing with her single sea-port in the White Sea, Austria might have much more readily effected by means of her harbours in the Adriatic. They are open at all seasons of the year; are equally well situated for communication with the trading marts of Europe, of Africa, and of Asia; and afford that natural outlet so essential for a country whose rulers cherish lofty designs, and which ought to take an important place in the history of the world.

Hemmed in by mountain ranges, and surrounded by powerful states, the prosperity and the safety of Austria depend upon facility of access to the sea. Deprived of this channel of communication with the commerce of the world, she would be at once shorn of half her strength. And to have possessed this line of coast, favourably situated in the Mediterranean, for so long a time, and to have altogether neglected the numerous advantages it offers, betrays a lamentable want of energy and discernment. Whilst Russia, France, Turkey, and even Prussia, have directed their energies to the development of the naval power, Austria alone seems to have been insensible to its importance.

The consequence is, that she has now to commence a work, that ought long since to have been completed. The other nations of Europe, on account of new inventions, are compelled to reorganize and in a great measure, to reconstruct their navies; the task Austria has before her is to create one. Any delay in the present altered state of affairs must lead to serious consequences.

Her resources for maintaining a prosperous commercial marine are so extensive, that it is surprising they should have been so long neglected. She possesses convenient ports, and abundant facilities for the creation of traffic. As a commercial marine affords the best foundation for a fleet for warlike and defensive purposes, the advance she has made, and is making in this respect must be greatly in her favour. Sailors are to be found in sufficient numbers amongst her own population, on the shores, and in the islands of the Adriatic. In fact, the materials are at hand, and all that is now required is prompt and decided action.

Happily much attention has been of late years devoted by her government to the improvement of internal communication, so that her varied products can be easily conveyed to the sea coast, while imported articles can be transmitted to the interior at a cheap rate. The improvement in her roads, and her rapidly increasing railway system, secure important advantages in this respect. So lately as April last, the direct line of railroad from Pesth to Trieste, was opened, by the Southern and Lombardo-Venetian Railway Company, and this route must materially enhance the value of their property.

And, what is still more important, the nucleus of the merchant marine already exists. In the limited commerce by sea, in which Austria has been hitherto engaged, about 10,000 vessels, most of them, however, of small capacity, have been employed. Her river, and sea traffic has been performed by seventy steamers, the average tonnage being under four hundred tons. Her royal navy consists of about fifty vessels, ten of which are steam-ships, none of them however of any size. As far as this branch of the marine is con-- cerned, the work must be entirely recommenced, if the empire is to assume that rank, as a naval power, to which she is by her position, as well as by her extensive interests, entitled. It is indeed a question of existence; she must either accept the requisite conditions, or renounce her claims to power.

I have in this chapter explained what I believe to be the chief desideratum of Austria. Elaborate arguments are not required, to enable an intelligent public to agree with me in the conclusion at which I have arrived. The matter is self-evident. The Emperor of Austria, the government, and the people are fully alive to its importance. One member of the imperial family has placed the subject in its clearest light. I think I may say that earnest efforts are being made to supply the deficiency. In the present emergency half measures will not answer; what is to be done, must be done well and at once.

CHAPTER VII.

THE LINE OF STEAM SHIPS FROM TRIESTE TO ENGLAND. (a)

Though much may have been sacrificed to negligence or delay, something may always be redeemed, by diligent efforts to atone for past omissions. Austria has discovered her mistake, and is labouring zealously to make amends. The truth had been forced upon her, that she must develope her naval resources. The prosperity of her people, the defence of her coasts, the integrity of her possessions, the extension of her foreign commerce, and her independence as a great power, depend upon the immediate adoption of this course of action.

This being admitted, the manner in which an object of such importance is to be accomplished becomes the next question for consideration. Are the measures for carrying out the improvement, calculated to command public confidence ? Much, doubtless depends upon the first step; I do not mean by the first step, the earlier efforts in Ministerial departments, the orders to do this or to do that, generally issued on a sudden emergency, but the first public act by

(a) The undertaking to which this chapter refers, is an ocean line of steam-ships which will shortly commence running between Trieste and England. As full particulars will be published in the newspapers, and other periodicals, I need scarcely enter very fully into the subject in this place.

which the new policy is inaugurated. It is this that will enable men to form an opinion on the chances of ultimate success.

It often happens that when any great change is to be accomplished, or any important undertaking carried out, differences of opinion prevail respecting what should be done. The mode of execution, as well as the point of departure, excite controversy. The case now under consideration appears to me to form an exception to the general rule. I do not imagine that any diversity of opinion can exist. Austria, like Peter the Great, must go direct to the fountain head. Her primary duty is to establish steam navigation between her principal port, and the centre of the world's commerce. She must put herself in communication with ocean trade and its innumerable interests. She is a non-naval power, and she must, therefore, be brought into closer connection with the leading maritime power of the universe. By this means she at once obtains markets for her varied productions, remunerative labour for her populace, facilities for forming a navy, a commercial marine, and opportunities for the improvement of her sailors. It is scarcely necessary for me to enumerate the incalculable advantages, that must flow from such a connection. They may be summed up as constituting everything that Austria requires, to give development to her resources, her influence and her power.

The situation of the Mediterranean sea, and this of course includes the Adriatic, which is indeed its chief arm, is so admirable, that in every period of history, one or other of its ports has formed a central mart for the commerce of the three quarters of the globe, the shores of which it washes. Ragusa, Genoa, and Venice have, each in turn, contended for the empire of the sea, whilst the first navies of which we have any record, sailed upon these well-known waters. Here, ocean commerce was, as it were, cradled and nursed into existence, and beyond the pillars of Hercules, or the Straits of Gibraltar, the earliest navigators did not venture to sail. It is under these circumstances, somewhat remarkable, that the discoveries and inventions of the present century, have not led to a revival of the prosperity of some of these Adriatic and Mediterranean ports. Improvements in shipbuilding, and the application of steam, as a motive power, have here, as elsewhere, produced a change, but the progression has not been so marked, nor so decided, as in other parts of the world. There is not a single port in the Mediterranean occupying to-day the position enjoyed by Venice or Ragusa, in the height of their prosperity. Nor can this be attributed to want of opportunity, or to the decay of trade. The commodities in request amongst civilized nations, are still found in this part of the world. It is the great high road to India and the East, and forms the centre, towards which those who desire either to purchase or to sell, naturally direct their attention.

An opening, therefore, of an unusual character presents itself, for the rise of another great commercial emporium, in this quarter of Europe. And from all the ports, whose inhabitants and rulers are endeavouring to secure for them the desired supremacy, Trieste undoubtedly bears away the palm. Nor has this fact escaped the notice of various enterprising men: In 1855, Mr. Charles F. Loosey, the Austrian consul general at New York, projected a line of steamers to ply between the United States and Trieste, from which the most important advantages were anticipated. It was proposed, by the establishment of regular communication by means of powerful ocean steamers, to connect the trading ports of the four quarters of the world; and there can be no doubt that innumerable advantages must have flowed from such an undertaking, had not the complications arising from the war, and the disturbed state of Europe, led to its abandonment.

The most glowing anticipations were formed by commercial men, both in America and in Europe, of the advantages to be derived from this project. And if this was the case with regard to an ocean line from Trieste to New York, how incalculable must be the benefits that will be secured, by a direct ocean line from Trieste to England, the real centre of maritime commerce! This will at once place a girdle round the world, connecting Trieste with all great commercial

E

states and cities, and securing for merchants of all trading countries, rapid and certain means of communication. It will supply in fact the link that has been so long wanting, to complete the circle of regular intercourse by steam with every railroad and shipping company in the world. It will bring an accession of traffic, and impart activity to many commercial interests, that have long suffered from stagnation.

The enlarged and economical commercial steam service, that will shortly be opened, between Trieste and England, must give an impetus to commerce which will be universally felt; and in this respect it commands and it deserves to command, the general support of the exporting community. But to Austria herself it is in reality the commencement of a new éra. It offers her opportunities for the creation of wealth, of which even its most zealous promoters have but a feeble conception. It will connect her with the activity, the enterprise, the trade of all civilized nations. It will open innumerable marts for her immense stores of natural productions, giving employment, and with employment, contentment, to the various races of which her empire is composed. This is indeed the restorer, of which her most ardent reformers have long been in search. And it will prove the parent of other undertakings of a similar character. The success of the ocean line to England, will show what are the real requirements of the Austrian empire, and how these requirements may be converted into prosperous enterprises. No sooner is a fresh outlet for capital discovered, than speculators, capitalists, and merchants, are eager to avail themselves of its advantages, flocking as earnestly to the new arena of their operations, as the gold diggers in Australia and California rush to some new and richer vein, or to some more prolific stream.

As a necessary and rapid consequence, the port of Trieste must immediately rise to the rank of one of the most influential marts of commerce in Europe; while trade at present directed into other channels, will at once return to its natural course. The accommodation afforded by the Southern and Lombardo-Venetian Railway, and the approaching completion of the Trieste Sissek line, which communicates with the Banat, will enable the port of Trieste to command ample supplies of grain. It will become the most convenient point for shipment to different European countries, and to England in particular. The resources of Trieste, properly developed, will secure for the producers in the corn-growing plains, watered by the Danube, certain, and easily accessible markets for their crops. Bosnia, Dalmatia, the Banat and Herzegovina will be truly opened up, while the inhabitants of Hungary and Transylvania will participate in the advantages of a steadily increasing trade. And the opening out of this trade will be the best olive branch that the Austrian government could offer to Hungary. To all classes of her people, whether landowners, tenants, small traders, or labourers, it must prove a constant source of wealth and improvement. Their isolated situation has proved the great obstacle against which this people have hitherto had to contend. Profits have been consumed in expense of transport, and a remunerative trade has been rendered all but impossible by the incessant interruptions in the traffic.

Foreign commerce creates an inland trade and moreover multiplies itself. Wherever large exports are made, imports of necessity follow. Trieste was at one time the centre of a flourishing commerce in foreign wares and productions, and though this has of late years, and from unavoidable circumstances, declined, the effect of a rapid, cheap, and direct commercial line of steam ships to England, will lead to its restoration. The proximity of the port to Egypt, independent of other important considerations, renders Trieste the best channel for rapid communication with British India. Were proper arrangements made, many passengers, and a considerable amount of goods would pass by this route. The position of the port is admirable. Situated in the south of Europe, it is within easy reach of both Asia and Africa, and appears in truth, to be expressly formed for the centre of ocean commerce in the Mediterranean and the Adriatic seas.

While the inhabitants of all portions of the Austrian empire, and every interest, whether political, financial, or commercial, must reap great benefits from the establishment of the line of steam-ships now referred to, I may mention particular undertakings, the prosperity of which will be increased to an almost unparalleled extent. The Southern and Lombardo-Venetian Railway, and the Austrian Lloyds are enterprises that admit of considerable extension. And I have no doubt that this ocean line from Trieste to England, will secure their natural and complete development.

The increase of traffic on the Southern and Lombardo-Venetian Railway, will raise the dividends to an amount that might, if stated, appear incredible. The capabilities of the line for traffic have not yet been put to the test. Everything travels by the northern route, finding outlets at Stettin, Hamburg, and Bremen. Take for instance one article of Austrian produce, grain, and it will be found that last year five million cwt. were shipped by the northern route, in the short space of two months, as reported by the *Times* correspondent! Yet the most prolific grain-growing districts are situated to the south, and the proper outlet for the bulk of this produce is Trieste. Nothing, but a well-organized system of ocean transport, is required to secure the shipment of this produce at its natural port. Had the grain, to which I have already referred, been conveyed by fast ocean steamers from Trieste, the Southern and Lombard-Venetian Railway must have received a large share of the profits derived from that exportation. Trieste, moreover, offers abundant accommodation for storing corn. The ocean line once established, large quantities would be accumulated in its granaries, and a certain market for the great staple of life would be at once formed. From this depôt merchants and importers could draw their supplies to meet the demand as it arose. Traffic increases the number of passengers on a line, because when large commercial transactions are carried on, speculators, merchants, traders and agents are continually passing from point to point. A railway is, moreover, greatly influenced by the condition of the population of the district through which it passes. In their prosperity the shareholders are certain to participate.

Nothing will tend so directly to create activity in all the provinces bordering upon the Adriatic, as rapid and regular steam communication with England. For all kinds of produce, good markets are at once secured. The inhabitants, from the necessities of trade, and their own improved circumstances, will move about much more frequently than at present, and both the passenger and the goods traffic of the Southern and Lombardo-Venetian line, will thereby increased beyond the most sanguine expectations of its directors. Nor is it only the produce of the neighbouring districts that will be conveyed by this route. For the larger portion of the Austrian dominions, the outlet at Trieste will prove more convenient, and less expensive, than ports closed by ice during the winter months.

In addition to the advantages already noticed, for the transport of grain, I may mention another of incalculable importance. It frequently happens that, as soon as the crops have been secured, and the grain is in a fit state to be forwarded to the markets beyond the sea, the ports through which it is now shipped are closed by the ice, and enormous losses are entailed upon the speculator. Hence the producer receives a much smaller return for his labour, than he might obtain if certain and regular means of transport were always at his command.

The advantages that must accrue to the Austrian Lloyds, placed by the ocean line to England, in direct communication with all the steam lines and railroads of the world, are self-evident. This company, like the Southern and Lombardo-Venetian Railway Company, will, I have no doubt, find a difficulty in providing means of conveyance for the freights collected at its various stations. The goods-traffic of both undertakings will be limited only, by their capabilities of transport. The result of this prosperity will be the creation of additional facilities in other directions, which will act as feeders to the older and better established undertakings.

CHAPTER VIII.

ADDITIONAL REQUIREMENTS.

The high position taken, and most justly, by Austria, at the Great Exhibition of 1851, the extreme beauty of many of her industrial products, and the number of prizes which she carried off, excited considerable surprise, more especially amongst that portion of the public who have not the slightest conception of the extent of her resources. Great changes have ensued since that memorable competition. Invention has carried improvement to an extraordinary pitch. Everywhere there has been rivalry. All the nations of Europe have been making the most strenuous efforts to occupy the first rank. Another trial of skill is approaching, at which Austria must exert herself, in order to maintain the position she has already secured.

The mighty agent, by which the most wonderful improvements have been effected, is steam. The application of its power, in a thousand different ways, has multiplied the resources of man, and imparted delicacy as well as strength to the work of his hands. One of the chief results, and most assuredly one of the greatest successes, which has followed the application of this power, is the annihilation of space, and the acceleration of intercourse between nations. Steam by land and sea, and the Electric Telegraph, are the most potent ministers of this age of commerce and civilization. They have bridged oceans, and converted desert regions into populous places. They have brought distant lands into close communication, and have enabled people dwelling in opposite quarters of the universe to become neighbours and friends. They have triumphed over what were once termed impossibilities, and enlarged the spheres of human enterprise and activity.

For these and other reasons, I have hitherto confined my remarks to the necessity that exists for the immediate establishment of communication by steamships, between Austria and the great markets of the world. The formation of the direct steam line between Trieste and England is undoubtedly the first step. There are, however, other measures the adoption of which will not only give additional value to this important improvement, but will enable Austria to establish other steam lines, that must have a material effect upon her prosperity and her influence, as one of the great powers of Europe.

Doubtless, the way has already been prepared by many salutary changes. Impediments to the free operations of trade have been in some instances removed. The customs-system, that separated

Hungary and other provinces from the rest of the empire, was abolished in 1851. The tolls on the Danube, and other rivers have been modified, and prohibition has been in some cases replaced by a protective tariff. Further reforms are, however, indispensable, and one of the most urgent has reference to the financial position of Austria.

The state of the currency has more to do with the sluggishness of trade in some parts of Europe, than legislators and political economists generally suppose. It is true that they are aware of the fact, that a restricted currency fetters the operations of commerce, but they have scarcely an idea of the extent of the mischief caused, or of the wonderful nature of the relief that remedial measures would secure. They perceive its fatal influences at work, in exchanges, and upon large commercial undertakings, but do not trace their paralysing effect upon the energies of those whose labour is their only capital; thus, in fact, making poverty and its attendant discontent, the sole birthright of a people.

Yet it is from this source,—labour, that the wealth of the capitalist, and, with that wealth, his power, invariably springs. His stores are the accumulation of numerous small rills, fed by the industry of those who earn their bread by the sweat of their brow. It is one of the first duties of every government to provide a circulating medium to answer the wants of the labourer, and of the small trader, as

well as those of the large capitalist. The former
require coin of small but of fixed and well ascer-
tained value; and the latter the means of making
large payments with facility. People, who have
transacted business in the different German states,
know how the want of certainty and of system inter-
feres with the operations of trade. The general
confusion that prevails, destroys confidence, and while
their capitalists appear at a disadvantage in the great
markets of the world, their operatives cannot turn
their labour to the best account. The true remedy
for this, is to be found in a well-regulated currency,
the selection of the best standard of value, and a
proper supply of the circulating medium.

Austria has suffered much from want of attention
to questions of this important character, and her
inability to resume cash payments was partially owing
to this cause. Silver is her standard, and but a small
quantity is in use. Without entering into arguments
respecting the necessity for a change in the legal
tender, it is evident that for an empire so extensive,
an increase in the gold coinage is required. The
course adopted by France, affords a strong illustration
on this point. In that country, as in Austria, silver
is the standard of value; and until very recently, that
is to say, within the last twelve years, only a small
quantity of gold was in circulation. The consequence was, gold coin was at a high premium. The
inconveniences caused by this scarcity became so

apparent that the French Government, availing themselves of the increased supply, obtained from the
mines of California, and Australia, provided and
issued a large quantity of gold coin. They did not
carry the reform to such an extent as to alter the
standard of value, but they relieved trade, and facili-
tated mercantile operations, by supplying a dangerous
deficiency in one portion of the circulating medium.

This salutary measure has, in a commercial sense,
proved the salvation of France. Had the sagacity of
her legislators failed on this point, she could not have
emerged with unimpaired credit from the bankruptcy,
and the prostration, into which she was plunged by
revolutionary troubles; much less could she have
borne the expenditure of the Crimean campaign, of
the expedition to China, or of the numerous public
works recently erected in so many parts of the empire.
This enabled her to surmount numerous embarrass-
ments, to enter upon a prosperous career, to amend
her tariffs, and to induce her people to look to trade,
as the surest source of wealth.

The influence of Austria, as one of the leading
powers of Europe, would be materially augmented
were she to provide a better and a more regular
supply of gold, without even going so far as to effect
a change in her legal tender. At present nearly the
whole of the gold coinage of Austria, is absorbed in
transactions with a few merchants at Galatz, Semlin,
Bucharest, and places on the lower Danube; and it

is not even sufficient for their limited trade. This metal is treated as an article of merchandise, and thus an unfavourable effect is produced in every operation in which her traders are engaged. This, in connection with its scarcity, in some degree accounts for the absence of mercantile activity in a country, which possesses all the elements required, to render it one of the most flourishing states of Europe. Moderate improvements in the currency of Austria, would be followed by immediate benefits; and were it possible for some general arrangement to be made in this matter, between all the German states, one decided advance towards that union, so essential for their welfare and security, would be obtained.

The encouragement of the Lottery Loans, which are regularly quoted on the Vienna Exchange, has a demoralising influence upon the people, and impairs the credit of Austria abroad. It is greatly to be desired that, in their earnest endeavours to effect a complete reform, the Austrian Government will abolish this fatal system. Though the apparent sacrifice of revenue may amount to £700,000 per annum, it will in the end be a great gain. A dangerous taste for gambling not only diverts money from channels in which it might be employed with general advantage, but encourages idleness amongst the people, and renders them unwilling, if not entirely unfit, to make any continued exertion.

Though the currency question is regarded with

indifference in some quarters, it is in reality second to none in point of importance. If commerce is to flourish, circulation must at least be free. I am afraid that the financial reformers of Austria lack boldness, or some more energetic measures would have been long since adopted. Nothing can, however, be accomplished in this direction without courage. Monopolists and usurers must be confronted, and their selfish aims frustrated. I look forward with anxiety to the happy day, when Austrian finance shall be elevated above the influence of grasping money-lenders, and narrow-minded cliques, who are altogether blind to their own interests, and placed upon an imperial basis. It ought to be made subservient to nothing but the general interest of the people.

In common with the other nations of Europe, Austria must revise her tariffs, and adapt them to an altered state of affairs. The old machinery has been everywhere discarded. Experience has proved, that as a source of revenue, low rates of duty are more productive than high charges. In order to secure this object, her statesmen will act wisely by commencing negotiations with England for a commercial treaty.

By liberal subsidies, she ought to encourage the formation of Steam-ship lines, and Telegraph Companies. They are the real pioneers of commerce, and in this age of activity, extended trade can only be obtained by their agency. I may mention two points, one having reference to the electric telegraph, and the other to the encouragement of ocean steam-ships, that will fully illustrate my meaning. By a proper attention to the requirements of the former, a considerable portion of the profits arising out of telegraphic communication between England and India, would be secured to Austria. And were adequate steam communication between Trieste and Alexandria, *via* Corfu, established, in connection with the ocean line from Trieste to England, by far the largest portion of the passenger traffic, provided the government made arrangements to convey passengers at cheap rates, or in other words established a third class commercial line between Great Britain and the East Indies, would be induced to take this route. Our traffic with India, China, Japan, Australia, and countries in the Pacific, is continually increasing, and the improvements in the means of intercommunication have scarcely kept pace with the requirements of the public. The day is not far distant when we shall have a direct overland route to India through the Austrian empire. At present an overland route to India is a misnomer. It cannot with justice be said to have been established, so long as the principal part of the journey is performed by steam-ships. The British and Austrian governments, however, have it in their power to open a real overland route, by which mails, passengers, and valuable merchandise would be enabled to reach India within eight days. Railroads already exist for about one-third of the distance. Were the communication completed, third class passengers might be conveyed at an expense of eight pounds sterling per head. Such an improvement in the means of communication can only be effected by a direct line of rail to the East Indies.

Were such a line established through a friendly state, the length of time consumed in the transit from London to Calcutta and other places in India, might be calculated with the same precision as in a journey to Paris. The long and difficult passage of the Red Sea would be avoided. The new route would speedily become the great highway to China, Japan, and Australia, and can alone meet the requirements of that important commerce which is now in its infancy. The increased traffic which this line must call into existence, would by setting in motion springs of industry that have hitherto lain dormant, render Austria from her central position one of the richest countries in Europe. In the mean time, as an auxiliary I feel assured, that a line of suitable commercial steamships to Bombay, Madras, and Calcutta for third class passengers, and light goods, viz: via Trieste and the Red Sea, would meet with very great encouragement from the public. It would be of such importance to Germany, and to Austria in particular, that the Emperor's ministers would act wisely were they at once to take measures for its early and permanent establishment.

The encouragement of mail lines, and the conclusion of postal contracts, would contribute to the prosperity of Austria. Whilst such extraordinary efforts, to provide necessary accommodation for the public in these matters, are being made by various European powers, this, the largest central state in Europe must suffer, if she does not actively follow the example of her peaceful rivals. Within the last few days, a small work has been placed in my hands, which contains ample confirmation of the justice of my views on the importance of subsidised mail steam-ship lines. It is entitled "United States and Mexican Mail Steamship Line, and Statistics of Mexico." The author, after alluding to the remarkable development of the commerce of Great Britain, that has followed in every instance in which mail steamers, with a liberal subsidy have commenced running, urges the Government of the United States to adopt the same wise plan.

From statistics in my possession, I can confidently assert that the development of commerce, consequent upon the establishment of mail steam-ship lines, is altogether unprecedented. In some places, exports that in no previous year had attained an increase of five per cent., were doubled in less than six years, after the mail steamers commenced their voyages. An ocean line from Austria to England, will set a thousand springs of industry in motion, and call forth new sources of wealth in different parts of the empire.

In England four hundred millions is invested in railways, those arteries by which the free circulation of commerce is maintained. In Austria railways have also been constructed, and nothing but the silver link—the bridge across the ocean, is required to connect these important channels of intercommunication. This once established, home industry will spring up, and foreign commerce, which gives value both to land and to labour, will revive. By such powerful aids the British people are enabled to pay the interest on the national debt, and to provide for their increased expenditure.

In this review of the additional requirements of the Austrian empire, I must not pass over one influence that is perhaps the most important of all, in shaping the destinies of a people,—I allude of course to the press, of which the Emperor's government has hitherto been so negligent. No state has suffered more from misrepresentation; none had more to gain from the dissemination of the truth. In the public opinion of Europe, Austria has in reality no representative, and therefore she has been completely abandoned to the attacks of her opponents. Many of the calumnies heaped upon her, the absurd stories circulated to her discredit, and the false accusations brought against her leading men, would have been neutralized, and swept away, had she possessed an impartial, and a disinterested organ to defend her cause against her numerous assailants. It is true that there are able and efficient journals within her own empire, but she cannot boast of a representative that commands the ear of Europe, or that can operate on the public opinion of the world at large.

Due attention to these and other matters, the introduction of machinery, the vigorous working of coal and other mines, the encouragement of trade and commerce, would secure to the various provinces of which the Austrian empire is composed, unexampled prosperity. Although these resources have been long neglected it is not too late to turn them to account. The people once convinced that great opportunities existed, would enter on the struggle of competition, and energy would prevail from one extremity of the empire to the other.

CHAPTER IX.

COMMERCE THE LINK REQUIRED TO CEMENT THAT
ALLIANCE BETWEEN AUSTRIA AND ENGLAND SO
ESSENTIAL TO THE WELFARE OF BOTH.

If there be two powers in Europe, that may be
regarded as natural allies, England and Austria are
those states. Interest in these matters is all powerful,
and there is not a single point on which their interests
come into collision. Austria maintains a large army,
England a small one; Austria does not possess a fleet,
England is the greatest naval power in the world;
Austria yields grain, wool, flax, hemp, tobacco, wine,
and other natural productions in abundance, and for
these England is obliged to become a purchaser on a
very extensive scale. Their interests are in fact never
opposed, if not altogether identical, hence the annals
of the past contain no record of wars between them.

There is in addition to all this a strong similarity
in the tastes and habits of the two people. During
the recent changes in the Government, the constitutional mode of proceeding, sanctioned by the example
and the practice of England, has been observed in
Austria. Our institutions, our laws, our literature,

are studied, admired, and in many instances imitated by the Austrian people. There is, in fact, a natural tendency towards friendship, and an intimate alliance. And this would have been formed and cemented, had it not been for the calumnies continually circulated through the press, by the enemies of Austria. Self interest is believed to be a strong motive. Yet how often do we see nations as well as individuals, committing themselves to a course that must prove not only detrimental, but positively ruinous, to the objects which they have most at heart! So it has been with England and with Austria. The people have suffered themselves to be misled by the enemies of both states, and have blindly pursued a line of conduct fraught with peril.

Truth will however prevail in the end, and even in the present case it would have vindicated its supremacy long ago, had the public, abandoning their prejudiced instructors, taken the trouble to inquire for themselves. When the people of England understand that an extensive trade with Austria only requires development, and when the inhabitants of the different provinces of that empire feel that the best markets for their produce is to be found in this island, they will quickly overcome the prejudices which have sprung up, and a better feeling will prevail on both sides.

The interests both of the English and of the Austrian people will be advanced by an intimate commercial alliance. Community of interest is the sole permanent bond of union between powerful states. Search through ancient and modern history, and you will not find endurance in alliances, that grew out of mere sentimental attraction, or were the development of an idea! The links that bind nations together are made of sterner stuff. The moment a shock comes, such insubstantial friendships vanish; whereas so long as a community of interests lasts, the true and natural alliance will endure. It often happens that nations, like individuals, are blind to their real interests, but let them once be enlightened on the point, and they will give their inclinations the right direction.

Austria offers, in addition to other advantages, food for our populace and employment for our mercantile marine; we give in return manufactures, the produce of our looms and of the spindles of Lancashire and Yorkshire, as well as the products of Birmingham and Sheffield, Leeds, Bradford, Manchester, Glasgow, Dublin, Belfast, and other important towns. What then can prevent an alliance between two states, that have nothing that can possibly create jealously or raise a controversy between them? They both have something to offer, and something to seek. By obtaining large supplies of grain direct from Austria, the drain of gold from this country will be checked, because Austria will take our manufactures, and employ our shipping in return. The balance of trade between the two kingdoms will be in fact restored.

As this proposed intercourse grows more intimate, other advantages must follow. Trieste will become the point of departure for India, and both Austria and England will be greatly benefitted by that result. The former country will be enriched by the trade arising from the constant traffic through her territories, and England will possess a direct route to her empire in the east, through a friendly state, and one whose friendship is not likely to be suddenly alienated.

From England, Austria may obtain the latest improvements in machinery, and learn how to utilize her immense stores of coal, and iron. She will moreover perceive, how the resources of a country may be increased, by the proper application of new powers. Her people, anxious to secure the rewards of honest toil, will willingly embark in the struggle, and by practice will gain an insight into the real value of labour, and its systematic sub-division. Thus their energies will be directed to the attainment of legitimate objects, and the general contentment which must follow will form the surest defence against the sophistries of greedy and rapacious agitators. Freedom of trade, freedom of internal circulation, and freedom of egress, and ingress—as one improvement naturally leads to another—may be speedily looked for.

I have not referred to the political advantages that might be secured, by zealous co-operation between the two powers, because the union I most strongly advocate, is that which has the development of commerce, and the maintenance of peace, for its principal objects. The more eagerly it is pursued, the stronger it will become, and the best guarantees for its preservation will be found, in the benefits it secures for the people and governments concerned. Let it once be fairly established, and all apprehension as to the result must disappear. If the whole community in both of these countries once appreciate its true value, no convulsion will be permitted to disturb a union so firmly and wisely formed.

The importance of such an alliance has been always recognised in this country, though it has not always been acted upon. Various obstacles have interfered to prevent the adoption of this policy in its integrity. Statesmen of every political school have borne testimony to its value. I do not desire to reproduce opinions current in bygone days, or I might fill pages with quotations, confirming my statement, from the writings and the speeches of some of our wisest legislators.

Even during the present session of Parliament, members of the Government, and members of the Opposition, have displayed a certain unanimity in their views, with respect to the services rendered by Austria in the great cause of European progression, and the high position which she fills, as a member of the European confederacy. During a debate in the House of Commons on the 7th of March, Mr. Gladstone observed: "When I speak of Austria, I

" draw a wide distinction between Austria in Italy,
" and Austria beyond it. Beyond Italy I wish her
" well with all my heart, and regard her as the main-
" stay of the peace and order of Europe."

On the same occasion Lord John-Russell remarked:
" I should be very glad to see Austria maintained,
" because I quite agree with my right honourable
" friend, the Chancellor of the Exchequer, that during
" many contests in Europe for two centuries past, we
" have often contended in the same cause, and against
" the preponderance of other powers, with Austria.
" I agree with him that Austria is a great, regular,
" and conservative power in the middle of Europe,
" that tends to preserve many of the political and
" social advantages which Europe enjoys."

In a remarkable discussion brought on in the
House of Lords, on Friday the 19th of April, by the
Earl of Ellenborough, similar views were expressed
by members sitting on opposite sides of the house.
Lord Ellenborough himself in the course of an
eloquent speech declared: "Austria, in her integrity,
" and in her strength, is absolutely necessary to the
" safety of every state in Europe. It would be im-
" possible to preserve the balance of power, if her
" integrity were assailed, and any man who entertains
" a desire of creating a war against Austria in
" Hungary, would be criminal in the presence of
" Europe, and the enemy of every man within its
" boundaries."

Grappling with the Italian question Lord Ellenborough, an ardent supporter of the emancipation of Italy, and of the new kingdom, remarked—" Austria " has not been fairly treated in this matter. At the " Congress of Vienna she gave up the Netherlands, and " in exchange received Italy, I say Italy, because though " Austria herself only got a portion of that country, " princes of the Austrian house, were established in " other portions, and it was perfectly understood that " it was the mission of Austria to maintain Italy against " the French. Genoa was given to Piedmont for the " same purpose. The Italian territory of Piedmont " was to be the advanced guard of Austria, against " France. That was the intention of the Congress of " Vienna. Whether it was a wise one or not, I shall not " now inquire, but with that intention Austria was established in Italy, and in endeavouring to maintain, " and extend her influence in that country she only " performed her original mission, and fulfilled obligations which she contracted in Vienna."

CHAPTER X.

The opening out, and the establishment of new markets in the centre of Europe, cannot fail to give an impetus to the prosperity of a commercial, and an industrial country like England. She requires not only markets for the different fabrics produced in such abundance, but also markets, in which her people may obtain those raw materials, which they know how to employ to such advantage, and to convert to so many useful purposes. It is in this respect, there-fore, that Austria presents such a field for enterprise. Her markets are invaluable, both to those who desire to purchase, and to those who have wares to sell. The vessel which carries out the produce of our looms, of our furnaces, and of our workshops, will return with food for our people, and with productions which will give employment to the labourer, the mechanic, and the artizan.

At this critical period, such a consideration is all important. Complications in both hemispheres, have already disturbed the balance between demand and supply, and many branches of trade, are unusually depressed. Our industrial population run some risk of not having sufficient work. This is, therefore, essentially a poor man's question; and more particularly so, in the manufacturing districts. America, temporarily excludes our wares from her markets, by rigorous tariffs. Her citizens have unfortunately exchanged the implements of peaceful industry for those of war. The wisest amongst us, can scarcely venture to assign limits to the quarrel which has now unhappily broken out, or to say how long the rupture may last. Be its duration long or short, and all philanthropists earnestly desire the speedy restoration of tranquillity, some time must necessarily elapse before commerce returns to its accustomed channels, and things are re-established upon their former basis.

The development of the immense resources of Austria, and the cultivation of our trade with that country, which would, under ordinary circumstances, and even in times of general prosperity, be objects worthy of our most anxious attention and endeavours, become at this moment of paramount importance. They afford a remedy, and the only remedy be it clearly understood, for evils, and perils that are rapidly gaining upon us. Mr. Canning, on a celebrated occasion declared, that he called the New World into existence to redress the balance of the Old. In like manner, it behoves our statesmen, our financiers, and our leading commercial men, to endeavour to call new markets into existence, to restore the balance so violently disturbed by the closing of olden marts, and to preserve that relationship between supply and demand, so necessary for the maintenance of prosperity in this, and in other countries of the world.

The question, moreover, is one that appeals directly, and eloquently to every interest, and to every class. To all who toil, it will secure increase of employment, and higher wages; to all who buy or sell, it will bring increased profits. Commerce, like mercy, is twice blessed, it blesses him that gives and him that takes. When it once springs up and takes root, no limits can be placed to the amount of good it accomplishes, or to the benefits it scatters among the people.

Though it is hardly necessary for me to enter into details on this point, I will mention certain interests, which will be more particularly benefitted, by the establishment of intimate commercial relations between Great Britain and Austria. And foremost amongst these is the capitalist, who of late years, has been sorely perplexed to find good investments. The undeveloped resources of the Austrian empire, offer extraordinary opportunities for the rapid realization of safe, and large profits. There are openings for the investment of capital, in various projects connected with that extensive empire, which might with care and under judicious management, be converted into mines of wealth. I hardly know of any country in which capital, under certain conditions, could at this moment be employed with so much advantage, and, what is more important still, in undertakings, the success of which has been tested in other states. Thus with experience as a guide, uncertainty is banished from the calculation, and the capitalist has only to do in Austria, that which has been done in other parts of Europe, in order to secure an ample return upon the money which he invests.

While many of our manufactures are suffering from stagnation, caused by an inadequate supply of the raw material, the advantages which Austria offers to this important interest, must be self-evident. As a producing country, she is altogether without a rival in this quarter of the globe. Whether the raw material required, be grain, timber, wool, hemp, flax, minerals, or the useful earths, a supply may be obtained from one or other of her provinces. The cotton and the woollen spinners of Lancashire and of Yorkshire, the hardware manufacturers of Birmingham, Sheffield, and other places, the proprietors of the Staffordshire potteries, and manufacturers of every kind in England, in Ireland, and in Scotland, will secure important advantages by availing themselves of the virgin markets of Austria.

Nor is it only as the storehouse of natural productions and of raw materials that Austria will prove so useful, but as a consumer. She will purchase the manufactured article, which she sent to this country in a raw state. Until her people obtain an adequate knowledge of mining operations, and this will require at least an interval of twenty years, her principal supplies of iron and of coal will be drawn from these islands. Milford Haven and South Wales must derive peculiar advantages from the opening out of this trade. In the Austrian markets there is a constant demand for English manufactures, and the more our traders buy of raw products, the more they will be able to sell of manufactured articles. Increase of trade will bring increase of wealth, for it is only the want of facilities, that prevents the inhabitants of Austria from taking a much larger quantity of English goods, than that which they at present consume.

The supplies of timber of all kinds that might be obtained from Austria, would have a beneficial effect upon every trade and handicraft in which wood is employed. This, therefore, is a question in which the builder, the shipwright, the furniture and cabinet-maker, and the cooper, have more than ordinary interest. The difficulty in obtaining well-seasoned wood for various purposes, is too generally known to require further explanation on my part. The activity of these, and of other trades, would receive a favourable impulse, from the increased demand that must necessarily ensue, and the aid of the ship-builder in particular, would be called in request, to enable Austria to construct a navy, and a mercantile marine. These

are objects on the possession of which her rulers have
set their hearts, and they are objects which all classes
in the empire are determined to obtain. Their importance as elements of power and of independence,
are fully recognised, and for their attainment the
efforts of Austria will keep pace with her means.

To our wine merchants, as well as our wine con-
sumers, Austria can offer advantages, which no other
European country has at command. The capabilities
of France, of Spain, and of Portugal, as wine producing countries, have been already tested, and from
certain provinces of the Austrian empire, a supply of
sound wine can be obtained to meet the increased
demand that has arisen from altered tastes, and more
liberal tariffs, of which Austria will not be slow to
avail herself. Imperfect means of intercommunication
and difficulties of transport have, hitherto, excluded
the rich vintages of Hungary, of Transylvania, and of
the Southern provinces from the English markets,
where, when they are once well known, they will
command a ready sale.

Foreign cattle enter largely into our consumption, and when cheap through rates by rail and steam-
ship, are established between Austria and England, our
graziers and purveyors will obtain large supplies of
live stock from different parts of the Austrian dominions. The breeding of horses has, also, been much
improved in that country, and large numbers of those
useful animals will be drawn from this source. Thus

the grazier, the horse-dealer, and the purveyor, will obtain a due share of the advantages to be derived from the establishment of closer relations with this country.

The question, in fact, as I before remarked, affects the interests of above sixty millions of people. It is one that appeals forcibly to members of every class, both in Austria, and in England. Taken in its true sense, it means increase of trade, increase of wealth, and increase of happiness. The three are links of a single chain—if one be lost, the others will soon be found wanting.

I have referred to certain interests that must receive an extraordinary extension, if the policy which I have advocated, be honestly and promptly adopted. I say promptly, because other nations are not altogether ignorant of the opportunity that presents itself, and by delay, our prospects will be imperilled. It is not only, however, certain interests, but the whole nation that will reap the benefit of the opening out of fresh sources of trade, and the establishment of a profitable commerce. Every man, both in Austria and in England, will find a greater demand, and consequently, a better market for his labour. It will be a boon to the masses, and by affording employment to the working population, will be a guarantee of contentment, and of continued prosperity, and progression.

G

CHAPTER XI.

It will not be difficult for the rulers and the
people of Austria, to obtain a clear and distinct
notion of the innumerable advantages, that must
immediately follow an intimate commercial alliance,
between their country and Great Britain. They have
but to look around them, and observe what trade, and
the industry it nourishes, have accomplished in other
directions. They need not examine into the records
of a past age, in search of a precedent; the process is
going on under their eyes. If they direct their
attention to Russia, and ask how it is that she is
enabled to maintain her position, and keep her
extensive empire together, they will be told that it is
by the cultivation, imperfect though it be, of trade.
If they inquire how France has been enabled to
recover from the prostration, consequent upon revolution and anarchy, and is able to bear an extraordinary
annual expenditure, they will be informed that it is

because a strong commercial element has arisen in that state. Even Spain, by the encouragement of trade, is enabled to make an effort that revives the glories of that era in her history, when her ships were found on every sea, and her colonial empire was the admiration of the world.

These, however, are only examples of what commerce imperfectly developed can accomplish. For its higher triumphs, and more extraordinary results, the rulers and the people of Austria, will do well to study the rise, the progress, and the commercial ascendancy of Great Britain. And if they desire to measure the question by a somewhat smaller scale, they may study the history of the United States of America. Possessing resources more extensive and various than those of any other European state, energy alone is required in the Austrian people, to enable them to turn their varied elements of power to the best account. The materials of wealth, and of influence, are accumulated in the different provinces of the Austrian empire; and the proper use and employment of these resources, will secure deliverance from present embarrassment, and a widely extending prosperity for the future.

For the purposes of trade, a more extended currency must be at once introduced, and this would give a death blow to that monopoly, which, as I have observed, is at this moment, one of the most grievous obstacles to the progress of Austria. The capitalist would no longer send all his money to foreign countries, but would find in undertakings at home, more legitimate channels for its employment. He would also obtain higher rates of interest, and thus be in every respect a gainer.

If these views are correct, one of the first effects of a better commercial system in Austria, would be to liberate the capitalist, and enable him to advance the welfare of his country, at the same time that he secured his own. The land-owners would obtain higher rentals, and would be thereby enabled to carry out improvements which are so essential for the proper development of the resources of the soil. In many parts of Austria, little attention is paid to cultivation. Regular markets, and adequate means of intercommunication, must secure enhanced prices, and these would act as an incentive to renewed exertion both in landlord and tenant. The owner and the tiller of the land would have a common interest. Persons who have travelled in Austria will understand, how much might be accomplished in this respect, by comparing the neglected state of some districts, which they must have noticed in their progress, with the high cultivation attained, between the Bavarian and the Saxon frontier, and the city of Vienna. There is ample room for improvement in many provinces, and the results attained in the localities to which I have referred, show what might be accomplished, so far as the cultivation of the soil is concerned, were inducements for the expenditure of capital, and the application of labour, afforded.

It is not only the grain grower who will be affected by the change. The producer of hemp, of flax, in fact of everything derived from the cultivation of the soil, would share in the prosperity that trade must create. One of the Austrian provinces, Bohemia, at present supplies the Paris markets with game. There would be a constant demand, and regular markets for whatever this rich country could produce.

Austria possesses many manufactures in which much skill is exhibited, and superior articles are produced, and yet they are shut out from the great marts of the world by wares of an inferior kind. This arises from the absence of that commercial activity, which would enable her producers to make the most of the advantages which they enjoy. Whatever increases price unnecessarily, must greatly prejudice, if it does not entirely arrest the sale. Manufacturers, therefore, whose welfare depends upon trade, are deeply interested in securing for themselves and their fellow countrymen, that extended commerce which will at once flow from freer intercourse with foreign markets.

At present the wine producer of Hungary, and of other provinces of the Austrian empire, has no foreign market for his growths. The quantity of wine that finds its way from the Austrian vineyards to other countries is so small that it is scarcely worth notice. Yet wine of excellent quality is grown, and in large quantities, and were ready access to the markets of Europe obtained, the quality might be much improved, and the produce increased, by more careful, and extended culture. I cannot believe that the Austrian wine grower will neglect the opportunity, which the reduction of the duty on wine by the English government, has placed within his grasp. Many of the wines produced in Austria, are of a character admirably suited to the tastes of the English people, and are better able than many continental wines to bear transport and the changes of climate. .

The timber, which abounds in her immense forests, and the minerals that are obtained from her extensive mines, might all be converted into sources of national wealth. And it is not only the actual possessors of these productions who would be enriched, were they turned to their legitimate use. It is the daily labourer, the man who earns his bread by the sweat of his brow, who would find a better reward for his toil. His condition would be improved, and he would be raised out of that of abject poverty, in which contentment is impossible.

I appeal, therefore, with confidence to members of every class in the Austrian empire. I advocate the interests of all, from the Emperor on his throne, to the peasant in his cabin. I know that one thought is ever present to the Emperor's active and enlightened mind, and that is, how he may secure the welfare and happiness of his subjects. I have endeavoured to point out a course by which I believe this may be accomplished. I have shewn that if trade is promoted, and facilities are afforded for increased traffic, prosperity will soon be established upon a firm basis. The inhabitants of the various provinces of Austria, will be induced to enter into the competitive struggle and to put forth all their energies. In this matter, interest and duty, go hand in hand. It is clearly the duty of every man to work energetically in the good cause of progress, and civilization. It is undoubtedly his interest to obtain a competency, if not to grow rich.

Commerce is the ladder by which states rise to eminence. If we consider which are the wealthiest, the most powerful, and the most highly civilized nations in the world, we shall find it is those states in which trade is most fostered, intercourse is most encouraged, and commerce is unfettered. Such nations enjoy the largest measure of intellectual as well as of material wealth.

CHAPTER XII.

REMARKS ON THE BALANCE OF POWER; AND GENERAL REVIEW ON THE SUBJECT.

That Austria possesses immense resources which only require development is sufficiently evident from the facts adduced in the foregoing pages. I have shewn what a future awaits her if her rulers follow, as I have not the slightest doubt they will do, the right path, and turn her capabilities to good account. And though I have passed in review some of the more important advantages that must accrue to England, and to Austria, from an alliance that is in reality one of the great requirements of this age of progression, I desire to offer a few remarks upon the general bearings of the question, and the benefits that it must confer upon the world at large. Much has been written and spoken upon the balance of power, yet erroneous views prevail on this subject and some modern politicians even go so far as to deny that the preservation of any such balance in Europe is a matter of much importance. A notion so erroneous must be attributed to want of proper information. Persons are too apt to consider, that the term balance of power is one of those convenient phrases which diplomatists have invented for interested purposes. They do not remember and perhaps they really are not aware, that it is the offspring of necessity; that it is one of those safeguards introduced into the European system, against real, and not imaginary dangers.

Its origin has been clearly traced by the great historian Dr. Robertson, and I feel that I cannot do better than refer to his testimony in support of its value.

When Charles VIII. of France, in 1494, marched at the head of his legions into Italy, he found nothing able to resist his progress. Florence, Pisa, Rome, and other towns opened their gates to the French soldiers and everything promised success to his ambitious schemes. As Robertson remarks, "The Italians quickly perceived that no single power which they could rouse into action, was an equal match for a monarch who ruled over such extensive territories, and was at the head of such a martial people, but that a confederacy might accomplish what the separate members of it durst not attempt." To preserve, therefore, the independence of the different states, the idea of the system of the balance of power owes its origin. It was the Magna Charta of the European confederacy, the real corner stone on which all their liberties rest.

In 1495, the Italian states combined for the preservation of the balance of power and with the aid of the Emperor Maximilian, and Ferdinand of Aragon they formed that confederacy which speedily relieved them from the yoke of the oppressor. "They had" as Dr. Robertson remarks, "extended on this occasion to the affairs of Europe the maxims of that political science which had hitherto been applied only to regulate the operations of the petty states in their own country. They had discovered the method of preventing any monarch from rising to such a degree of strength as was inconsistent with general liberty, and had manifested the importance of attending to that great secret in modern policy, the preservation of a proper distribution of power among all members of the system into which the states of Europe have formed themselves. During all the wars of which Italy was at that time the theatre, and amidst the hostile operations which the imprudence of Louis XII. and the ambition of Ferdinand of Aragon carried on in that country, with little interruption from the close of the fifteenth century to the period at which the subsequent history commences, the maintenance of a proper balance of power between the contending parties, became the great object of attention to the statesmen of Italy."

Having clearly pointed out the origin of the important principle and its application in one particular direction, the historian comments upon the results of its use in a more extended sphere. "Nor was," Dr.

Robertson continues, "the idea confined to them. Self-preservation taught other powers to adopt it. It grew to be fashionable and universal. From this era we can trace the progress of that intercourse between nations which has linked the powers of Europe so closely together, and can discern the operations of that benevolent policy which during peace, guards against remote and contingent dangers and in war has prevented rapid and destructive conquests."

Such then was the origin, and such the progress of that benevolent policy which enabled different European nations to become great, without trenching upon the rights of others, and which for four centuries has formed a permanent bond of union. No sooner were its numerous advantages recognised and appreciated, than the policy was at once accepted. The germ might appear insignificant, the results however, soon shewed what a mighty change had been accomplished. The conclusion of the celebrated league of Venice, March 31st, 1495, was the first act in this auspicious change. Its authors had but a faint idea of the benefits they were conferring upon mankind. While they were carrying on their conferences by night, and doing all they could to keep the matter secret, they little imagined that the principles on which they were acting, would speedily become the guiding policy of Europe. The necessity for preserving the balance of power was gradually acknowledged. At the pacification of Europe, settled by the treaty of Westphalia, Oct. 23, 1648; the principle of the preservation of the balance of power was received as a fundamental part of international law. And from that day to this, it has proved the sole defence of the weak against the rapacity of the strong, and the best safe-guard of modern progress and civilization.

Those who have traced the origin of this policy cannot fail to be familiar with the innumerable benefits which it has during the last three centuries secured to Europe; and those who understand the nature of the perils with which modern civilization is even at this hour menaced, will not be led astray by the fallacy, that this international understanding is an empty expression. This restraint once removed, war becomes inevitable, and one of the first essentials of its preservation is the maintenance of the Austrian empire in full strength and integrity. She stands as a barrier between France and Russia—a barrier which every European kingdom, and England in particular has the deepest interest in upholding.

Occupying the position she does Austria should be strong, and the surest way to add to her strength, is by enabling her to develope her resources. Were this once accomplished the panics by which commerce is now too frequently paralysed would cease, because Austria would wield her rightful influence in the councils of Europe, and that influence would be exerted for the preservation of peace. The wealth, and the activity to which extended trade must give rise would at the same time afford her people the strongest interest in maintaining a peaceful policy, and render them dangerous to those who sought to disturb the general harmony in the pursuit of selfish aims or schemes of special aggrandizement.

As one of the great powers of Europe, the influence of Austria must be materially augmented by a liberal policy both in her political and her commercial system. This will be best attained by the adoption of measures such as those which I have advocated, and which I am happy to say are being adopted, and I therefore feel justified in considering my views for the development of the resources of this influential empire, calculated to render it a powerful agent in the good cause of progress and civilization. It is something in the furtherance, and in the success of which all Europe, and even the world at large, have an interest, and as such I look forward with confidence to the result.

We may now once more turn our attention from that aspect of the question in which the balance of power in Europe and the general well-being of the world are concerned, to the consideration of the advantages that must accrue to particular powers and interests. This again brings us to the benefits to be derived by both countries, from the conclusion of a treaty of commerce between England and Austria, and the establishment of an active trade.

To Austria herself the gain will be incalculable—

it means life, activity, energy, instead of embarrassment, decrepitude, decay. By being placed in direct
communication with the first naval and manufacturing
country in the world, an impetus will be imparted to
every interest in her widely extending dominions.
She has but to follow the example of England. By
substituting motive for animal power, and by availing
herself of the aids of invention, and enterprise, she
has multiplied all her resources. Her power is not
limited by the number of her population. New
agents have been called into existence, and the thirty
millions of people are served by hundreds of millions
of inanimate producers.

It is impossible that the advantages to which I
have referred, can be much longer neglected. I call
upon the people of England, the people of Austria,
nay, even the inhabitants of Europe to make some
use of the opportunities offered them, to turn to
account the mines of wealth lying at their feet. Open
the map of Europe, and observe the position occupied
by Austria! Consult any source whence trustworthy
information may be obtained; and you will learn
what treasures are buried in her territories. Draw a
line from her ports in the Adriatic to the great centre
of the world's commerce, England, and you trace a
channel which once opened, will by the facility it
affords for the constant interchange of products, add
to the riches and to the gratification of mankind!

And how shall I describe the increase of wealth and

power that additional means of intercommunication must secure to Austria herself! How can the benefits which that connecting link with the great world will ensure be enumerated or described? I have already pointed out a few of them. It will call forth activity from one end of her dominions to the other. It will set in motion the fertilizing current of trade and industry that has long been frozen up. It will place before men the objects that induce them to enter into the struggle of honourable competition. It will be to Austria not only a source of wealth, but an element of power. It will enable her to enter upon that active life by which alone the progression of a great empire can be maintained. The Austria of the past may be compared to a giant asleep, the Austria of the future, if these changes are fully and fairly carried out, will be a giant aroused, exercising all his energies and putting forth all his strength.

www.ingramcontent.com/pod-product-compliance
Lightning Source LLC
Chambersburg PA
CBHW031440270326
41930CB00007B/801